To: _____

From: _____

LiFe

SIMPLE DIRECTIONS FOR FINDING YOUR WAY

MaPS

GREGORY E. LANG

CUMBERLAND HOUSE
NASHVILLE, TENNESSEE

LIFE MAPS
PUBLISHED BY CUMBERLAND HOUSE PUBLISHING, INC.
431 Harding Industrial Drive
Nashville, TN 37211

Cover design: James Duncan Creative, Nashville, TN
Text design: Lisa Taylor
Cover photograph: Getty Images
All photographs except those on pages 51, 64, 100, 106, 149, and 167 by Gregory E. Lang

ISBN-13: 978-1-58182-522-0
ISBN-10: 1-58182-522-6

Printed in the United States of America
1 2 3 4 5 6 7 — 11 10 09 08 07 06

To my wife, Jill, and my daughters, Meagan and Linley.
May we always walk hand in hand along a long and peaceful road.

Introduction

OVER THE YEARS I have had the delight of watching my daughter, Meagan Katherine, reach many milestones. I will never forget the first time she called me "Daddy," her first steps, and when she became potty trained. Her words "I can do it" were spoken with insistence; she wanted the chance to accomplish by herself whatever the task at hand. I was thrilled to see my little girl growing up yet also happy that she still wanted to hold my hand, ride on my back, and give me kisses.

As these early years passed and she continued to grow, other milestones approached and new tasks required mastery. Some I could just demonstrate for her, like how to tie her shoes, buckle her seatbelt, and use the microwave oven. Others required a bit of practice and explanation, as when she wanted to make her own scrambled eggs, shuffle a deck of cards, and later, use a computer. As my daughter grew up and became more independent and less willing to turn to me for what she wanted and needed, I began to feel the sting of loss. Too soon it seemed I was no longer needed to read her to sleep, walk her to class, or help her with her homework. All too quickly she entered her preteen and then teenage years. I knew other milestones were ahead and new life tasks would challenge her, but by now she had begun to turn more often to her mother for guidance, and I struggled to find a place in her life.

One afternoon while visiting my parents, who live on a remote country road, Meagan and I went for a drive. She was at the wheel. She had been driving in open fields for two years by then, an activity meant to give her as much driving experience as possible before she set out by herself without Dad by her side to make sure she was safe. On this day I unexpectedly found myself requesting that my young driver turn off the familiar road and onto an unfamiliar one—and then another and another.

Soon she had driven much farther than she ever had before. She was frightened when she first pulled into traffic but smiled eagerly at the same time. She listened intently as I gave instructions and advice, following my directions without complaint or rebuttal. She beamed at me when I praised her as she skillfully negotiated the roadway. Under my tutelage she was learning something new. It reminded me of earlier times. I knew something she wanted to know, and she needed my help to master it; she needed me.

I decided that afternoon that driving was the bridge I needed to reach out to my daughter again, to have the occasion to spend time with her in the way that I missed, having fun together, laughing large, and teaching her something that would prepare her for the day when she would set out on her own. For the next three years we practiced driving every chance we got—driving in the rain, after sunset, practicing parking and hard braking, and learning how to intuit other drivers' moves. I helped her study for the learner's permit test. I was with her when she took it and tried to calm her nerves as we waited for her results. A great sense of accomplishment came over me when she proudly held her permit up for me to see, and in that moment I was where I wanted to be—in her favor, basking in the warmth of her smile.

Meagan now drives nearly every time we get in the car. It was on one of our first extended drives that the need arose for teaching her about road maps. We were taking my eleven-year-old stepdaughter, Linley, to summer camp, and I did not know the way. I spread a state map out on the dining room table and proceeded with Meagan at my side to find a route. We began by looking up our destination in the index then followed the grid lines to pinpoint it on the map. Once located, we surveyed the various roads we could take from our home to that tiny dot. We settled on a route that included city streets, interstate highways, two-lane mountain roads, and finally, a winding dirt road. We chose an alternate route for coming back, one that wound through the countryside, taking us through little town after little town and eventually home. Meagan was excited; it would be the longest time she had ever been behind the wheel.

The morning of our departure arrived. The girls and I rose early and had breakfast at a local diner before heading toward the mountains. Linley got some extra sleep in the backseat while I navigated for Meagan. For the next three hours she and I followed the directions we had written down. I helped her recognize the landmarks we were looking for, coached her on keeping up with the distance between turns, and taught her that even-numbered interstates ran east-west while odd-numbered ones ran north-south. Suddenly she asked me what to do if she ever got lost. I reminded her of her cell phone and then opened the glove box to show her the road maps I keep tucked away in there.

The three of us embraced before leaving Linley at camp, and then Meagan and I set out on our return route home. We listened to music, drove with the windows down, had lunch at a roadside barbeque joint, and stopped to shop at an old country store complete with a few old men in overalls sitting in rocking chairs on the front porch. We were having fun. Once back on the road we encountered a detour and had to refer to our map again. We selected a new route for the last leg home and continued on our journey.

As Meagan drove she remarked once more that she worried about becoming lost, that she needed to practice using a map. I realized then that I had less than a year to teach my child all I wanted her to know before she became fully licensed and able to drive off without me alongside to help her find her way. I imagined her going into the world alone, driving to her first job, leaving for college, going on road trips with friends between semesters, hoping she would not lose her way. I thought of all the things I wanted to warn her about, the things I wanted to make sure she could handle, and the many other life tasks she would need to master on her own one day.

As I looked out the car window, the old sting of loss and worry about her eventual departure came back to me. I know I have to let my child go. I cannot keep her under my wing, not that she would she let me. Yet I asked myself, *How do I let my daughter go before I am certain she is ready for what she will face? How do I prepare my stepdaughter, Linley?* I thought of Meagan's fear of becoming lost and my own fear of her losing her way. I suddenly wanted to write down some directions for driving, even for *living*, and stuff them into the folds of the maps in the glove box. I smiled as I imagined her pulling off the road one day to refer to a map, unfolding it, and having my hand-scribbled notes fall into her lap. "Don't drive too fast," "Follow at a safe distance," "Keep a diary," "Laugh often," and "Come home now and then," they would say.

In that moment the idea for this book came to me. Better a book than random notes in the glove box, I thought, because she could keep a book at her desk, on her nightstand, in her briefcase, or anywhere else close at hand, ready and waiting for her when she wants to reminisce about what we have done together, when she wants to know how much I care about her, or when she needs a hug and I am not near enough to give it to her.

And so here it is, this book that might have been notes tucked away in a road map, a collection of fatherly advice and directions for living a wonderful life, offered with love to my little girls. Meagan, I hope you will read it when you get lost, when you just want to reassure yourself of where you are going, and when you miss me. And Linley, put your shoes on; we are going for a drive. You take the wheel.

LIFE MAPS

1. Keep a current local map and U.S. road atlas in your car.

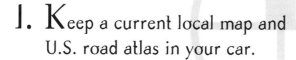

2. Remember to use your turn signals. It is important to let others know what your intentions are.

3. Keep a flashlight in your trunk. Make sure it has working batteries.

4. **W**rite down your directions in large print
before you go rather than trying to read
a map while driving.

5. **T**ry not to drive with less than one-quarter of a
tank of gas. You can't always count on finding a gas
station when you need one.

6. **A**lways follow others at a safe distance. You
never know what they may suddenly do.

7. **W**hen you are tired, take a break. Pushing yourself beyond your limits can be dangerous.

8. **P**lan your route ahead of time and plan an alternate just in case.

9. **D**on't play your music so loud that you cannot hear what is going on outside of the car.

10. **S**tay out of other drivers' blind spots.

11. **B**uy a camera and use it as often as possible.
Get extra copies of the pictures
and give them to others.

12. **V**isit historic places and keep a travel
journal of your experiences.

13. **T**here is a lot to see in this world. Go to a
different place every vacation.

14. Be independent. Running with the pack isn't always the best decision.

15. Make time now for those who love you. You never know how much time you might have to give later.

16. Loyalty begets loyalty. Be loyal.

17. Contribute time and money generously when you can. When you cannot, make up for it later.

18. Reciprocate every act of kindness and pay it forward.

19. Understand that every trespass doesn't call for a response. Sometimes it is best simply to do nothing.

20. Live by the Golden Rule every day.

21. Even if you don't think you need to, watch what you eat.

22. Don't weigh yourself every day. You'll drive yourself crazy.

23. Don't let your kids eat junk food. Eating healthily is a habit that must be formed as early as possible.

24. Don't eat reduced-fat foods.
Just eat less of the real stuff.

25. Tip at least 20 percent, sometimes
more for really good service. You'll be
remembered on your next visit.

26. Learn how to poach an egg. It's impressive.

27. Buy cheap bottled water.
It tastes just like the pricey stuff.

28. Have a compass so that you know where you are headed. Have a moral compass, too.

29. Bring surprise gifts home now and then. It will make a huge difference in a loved one's day.

30. Write letters to those you love. Your words will be treasured.

31. Pray out loud. It is helpful to listen to yourself.

Psalm 13

Psalm 16

A miktam[d] of David.

[1] Keep me safe, O God,
for in you I take refuge.
[2] I said to the LORD, "You are my Lord;
apart from you I have no good thing."
[3] As for the saints who are in the land,
they are the glorious ones in whom is a...

He who does these things
will never be shaken.

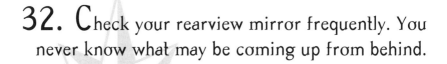

32. Check your rearview mirror frequently. You never know what may be coming up from behind.

33. Always wear your seatbelt; wear it properly.

34. Keep some spare change in your car.

35. Keep notepaper at hand so you can write down important thoughts before you forget them.

36. Keep an extra key hidden on the car. You will need it one day.

37. When stopped at a traffic light, always pause a moment when your light turns green. You never know when someone else may try to beat their red light.

38. When on long trips get out and stretch now and then. If traveling with someone, take turns driving.

39. Yield to pedestrians.

SLOW
CHILDREN
AT PLAY

40. Learn how to play at least one sport. You don't have to be good at it, just able to play it.

41. Listen to your doctor. Ask lots of questions.

42. It's true—you need to see a dentist twice a year.

43. Take your medication only as directed.

44. Draw up a living will and give copies to key people in your life.

45. Never buy a home without having it inspected first.

46. When the cashier asks for your phone number, feel free to politely say "no."

47. Don't be lured into a "get rich quick" scheme. If it worked, it would be the well-guarded secret of a *really* rich person.

48. Never sign a contract you
don't understand.

49. Don't follow your minister blindly.
He is human, too.

50. Always congratulate those who beat you at
something. It's good sportsmanship.

51. You cannot always rely on your own judgment. Ask for advice from those you trust.

52. When in doubt, wait. Often a quick decision is the wrong one.

53. Be careful when "reading" someone's body language. They may not use the same language you do.

54. Always tell the truth and expect the same from others.

55. Give more than you take. It will come back to you one way or another.

56. Learn to love others before yourself. They will then love you more than you ever could.

57. Do not always judge a book by its cover, but at the same time realize that sometimes all you need to see is the cover.

58. Never pull away from a hug.

59. Be able to recite from memory at least one romantic poem.

60. Reach out and touch someone you love when the opportunity presents itself.

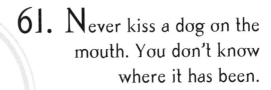

61. Never kiss a dog on the mouth. You don't know where it has been.

62. Never lie about your age. It's okay to fudge a little about your weight.

63. Change your hairstyle once in a while.

64. Never pet a rabid dog. That goes for people, too.

65. Be careful following the latest self-help fad. They sometimes lead to self hurt.

66. Seek counseling in times of marital discord. Both of you will benefit from a fresh, objective perspective.

67. Try harder when given a second chance.

68. When you feel like crying, do.

69. Clean breaks heal faster. When a relationship is over, let it be over.

70. Understand that when your children create distance from you, it is a normal developmental process. They will come back.

71. Forgive your parents for their mistakes. They meant well at the time.

72. Never take up a habit that you know you will need to break someday.

73. Whenever you are near the beach,
go put your feet in the water.

74. Make a fool of yourself once in a while.
Being serious all the time is exhausting.

75. Get some sun but use a good sunscreen.

76. Always wear shoes when using
a lawnmower.

77. When you have done something wrong, don't try to get out of it. Facing consequences is a part of living.

78. Be trustworthy. It is an honor to be trusted.

79. Be transparent, not mysterious.

80. Be comfortable with yourself. It isn't necessary to be like everyone else.

81. Don't get bogged down in a swamp
of secrets. You may not find your way out easily.

82. Do not use others for your own benefit
unless you want a very small circle of
short-term friends.

83. Remember that succeeding in marriage
and family is better than becoming the
world's best CEO.

84. Know how to change a flat tire.

85. Observe all things in your surroundings not just what is directly in front of you.

86. Comply with the maintenance schedule of your car. You must take care of things to make them last.

87. When someone you know is in need,
extend your hand.

88. Be the first to greet the newcomers to your
neighborhood. Take along a homemade treat.

89. Be thankful for what you have and waste
none of it.

90. Do not let a chance to say
"thank you" pass you by.

91. Donate the things you don't use.
Someone else needs them.

92. When you have overnight guests, give them
the nicest towels you have.

93. When you give a book as a gift, always
write a personal message inside.

94. When invited over for dinner,
always take flowers or a bottle of wine.

95. Don't be taken in by a well-rehearsed sales pitch.

96. Spend less money than you've got and don't spend what you haven't got.

97. Price doesn't always equal value or taste. Avoid spending your money just to impress.

98. If the salesperson keeps trying to lead you somewhere you don't want to go, walk away.

99. Buy only term life insurance.

100. Never buy the extended warranty protection plan.

101. Money can be attractive, but it doesn't age as well as good companionship.

102. Stay in touch with those who care about you. They like to know you are well.

103. Stay in touch with those you love. They'd like to hear from you more often than you think.

104. Never turn down your child's offer to help you.

105. Never turn your back on your friends and family.

106. Read instructions carefully and completely, even if you think you know what to do.

107. Keep a plunger in every bathroom of the house. No one wants to go searching for one when it is needed.

108. Don't be totally dependent on repairmen. Learn how to fix some things yourself.

109. Keep emergency contact numbers in your wallet.

110. Keep an extra key hidden outside your house but in a hard-to-find place. If you end up having to tell someone where it is, move it to another hard-to-find place.

111. Limit clothing purchases to those with care labels that read "dry clean only" or "machine wash, tumble dry." You'll soon hate the "hand wash only" kind.

112. Don't forget to stop and smell the roses—literally. Watch the sun rise, too.

113. Always give thanks, for what you have has indeed been given to you.

114. Live in the moment to get the most from it and plan for the future at the same time to get the most from it, too.

115. Smile and wave at strangers. You might make someone's day.

116. Become an expert at mending fences.

117. Tell your personal story
when given a chance. Someone will
learn something from you.

118. Give praise often. Your encouragement may
motivate someone who needs it.

119. Resist the temptation to become inebriated
with the exuberance of your own verbosity.

120. Be a parent for your children,
not their best friend.

121. Read about child development and learn
what to expect before you become a parent.

122. Don't give your child a name
that can be shortened to something embarrassing
or made fun of.

123. Don't have double standards. If you don't want the kids doing it, you shouldn't do it either.

124. Treat your children as equitably as possible.

125. Make sure children understand that being angry at them doesn't mean you don't love them.

THANK YOU

126. Keep "Thank You" notes on hand.
Use them often.

127. Make sacrifices for those you care about,
especially your children.

128. Honor your family traditions
and start new ones.

129. Resist the temptation to exploit someone's
weakness for your gain.

130. Every disagreement need not be won.
Learn how to choose your battles.

131. Those who are older are usually also
wiser and more experienced.
Listen to them. Learn from them.

132. Don't leave others guessing. Say what is on
your mind. Say it with diplomacy.

133. Try to be the first to say "I'm sorry." It will bring conflict to an end much sooner.

134. Never leave someone thinking, *I have no idea what she was trying to say.*

135. Keep your eyes and ears open for new opportunities.

136. Stretch your limits once in a while. You may find you have more range than you thought.

137. Your family is your most important asset. Make sure everyone knows you think so.

138. Keep an address book of all your relatives' addresses and phone numbers. Use it often.

139. Say "Happy Mother's Day" and "Happy Father's Day" to your in-laws, too.

140. It is more important to care about what your loved ones think than what strangers think.

141. Give a child a ride on your shoulders.

142. Give your affection freely.

143. Be affectionate with your spouse in front of your children so they will know what true love looks like.

144. Be penitent when you have caused others harm or inconvenience.

145. Don't believe your own story if no one else does.

146. Remember that the best advice is that which is asked for.

147. Pitching a fit usually doesn't get you very far. Learn to complain firmly but politely.

148. Remember that it is never too late
to ask for forgiveness.

149. Be scrupulously honest in all dealings,
especially those that involve love or money.

150. When there is enough blame to go
around, always take your fair share.

151. Never return something you
have used and pretend that you haven't.
That's cheating the merchant.

152. Keep a list of things to do. When you feel bored, work from the list.

153. Don't be a pack rat.

154. Do not procrastinate. It keeps you from getting things done.

1. Change oil
2. Wash car
3. Reservations
4. Directions
5. Snacks
6. Film
7. Phone #
8. Pack

155. Work to improve your writing skills. The ability to write a good letter or proposal is a valuable asset.

156. Stay in college at least until you have earned a master's degree.

157. Never stop learning. Take a night class or read a how-to book.

158. Always get your business agreements in writing.

159. Get a little culture. A broad fund of knowledge and range of experiences will add to your success.

160. Set goals. Write them down. Pursue them. Reward yourself when you achieve one. Then set a new one.

161. Always stand during the national anthem.

162. Put an American flag on your house. Never leave it outside in the dark or rain.

163. Visit a veteran's cemetery on Memorial Day.

164. Show respect for public servants.

165. Register to vote when you turn eighteen and be sure to vote in every election.

166. Speak openly about your faith and listen as others tell you of theirs.

167. Pray regularly, more often when you are a parent.

168. Commit yourself to a church that funds missions, not buildings.

169. Respect other people's religious beliefs. Engage them in conversation, not debate.

170. When someone you care about needs to vent, let them.

171. Ask someone to change something about themselves only if you are willing to change something, too.

172. Try to be logical, not just emotional.

173. Be nice to strangers. You never know in what setting your paths will cross again.

174. Do not unload all your problems at one time on one person.

175. Be honest about your intentions. Never mislead someone for your own pleasure or gain.

176. Show some grace when others have offended you.

177. Never lie. You will get caught, sooner or later.

178. It is easier to lose someone's respect than it is to earn it. Once it's earned, be sure to keep it.

179. Become skilled in the art of saying "no" with style.

180. Don't try to always be in charge but take charge when no one else will.

181. If you have led someone to expect something from you, don't get mad at them when eventually they do.

182. Don't ask for or seek pity.

183. Recognize that everyone will not like you. Don't be bothered by it when someone doesn't.

You are loved

184. Make a daily habit of telling someone "I love you."

185. Avoid comparing your current love to former ones. Let each stand on their own.

186. Kiss someone when they least expect it.

187. Learn the meaning of and obey all traffic signs.

188. Remember that speeding rarely gets you anywhere faster.

189. Always check your mirrors and gauges before driving off.

190. Slow down in rain and snow and proceed with caution.

191. Shift into a lower gear when going down steep hills.

192. Try not to get impatient with other drivers. They may be beginners or just lost.

193. Familiarize yourself with the legend of your road map. It will help you get where you are going and anticipate what's ahead.

194. Remember, the highway is not the place for aggression.

195. Learn how to swim.

196. Take a multivitamin every day,
one packed with antioxidants.

197. Eat fresh fruits and vegetables every day.

198. When you are sick, stay home.
No one else wants what you have.

199. Be accepting of those who are
different from you.

200. When given a chance to walk in
someone else's shoes, do it.

201. Diversify your portfolio, your work
experience, and your social circle.

202. Consensus is great when you can get it, but you can't always. Be prepared to make an executive decision.

203. Don't stand by a bad decision.

204. Trust your lawyer, your doctor, your mother, and your spouse.

205. Always dress appropriately for the given occasion.

206. Rather than wait for someone to come to you, go to them.

207. Learn the art of conversation. Practice it often.

208. Use humor to lighten heavy conversations.

209. Loving someone is all the more reason to tell them when they are wrong.

210. Plan for the unexpected so that you aren't taken off guard when something unexpected happens.

211. Look over your shoulder occasionally to see where you have been. Don't forget from where you have come.

212. There will be fender benders in life. Take them all in stride.

213. Believe that you were created with intent, not by accident, and then go on and find your purpose.

214. Pay attention to where you are going. When you see that you are headed in the wrong direction, turn around before you have gone too far.

215. When you think your life is unbearable, remember that there are people all over the world who would gladly trade places with you.

216. Your children will say and do things that will hurt you. Love them most during those times.

217. Ask your children lots of questions. Everything they do is your business.

218. Always let your children know how important they are to you.

219. Do what is right for your children, not just what will make them happy.

220. Should you have stepchildren one day, adopt them if you have the option.

221. Allow your children to explore and take risks. It builds their confidence.

222. Don't expect your children to be just like you.

223. Be someone that others can lean on in times of need or sorrow.

224. Always call someone back if you said you would.

225. Do not let success go to your head. It will lead to failure.

226. Sometimes carelessness follows confidence. Don't get too confident.

227. Always keep your resumé current.

228. Say only good things about your boss. Anything else will get back to her.

229. Choose a job that complements your personality.

230. Don't lose touch with your favorite co-workers when you change jobs.

231. Be honest on your resumé and then sell yourself during the interview.

232. Prepare yourself to get the job that will allow you to give your children what you want them to have.

233. Keep your workspace neat. Neatness is a sign of organization. Organization is a sign of promotability.

234. Always have something near at hand to read.

235. Keep a journal. You may not read it for years, but when you do, you'll be glad you wrote things down.

236. Recognize that no one individual can be an expert in everything, so have several resources to turn to.

237. Stay in the center of your lane. Drifting too far to the right or left can be dangerous.

238. When driving in heavy traffic, keep distractions to a minimum, including phone calls.

239. Never trust someone's blinker. They may not even realize it's on.

240. When having car trouble, always pull completely off the road. Stop in full view of others.

241. When accepting help from others, be gracious but also be cautious.

242. Learn how to parallel park. Practice until you become an expert at it.

243. When you have passengers, remember you have taken their lives into your hands. Proceed responsibly.

244. When you are a dinner guest in someone's home, always offer to help clean up afterward.

245. If you wake up on the wrong side of the
bed, take care not to ruin the morning
for everyone else.

246. When hosting a dinner party, make sure
you know if any of your guests have allergies.

247. When a guest in someone's home, observe their customs.

248. Eat at least one bite of everything someone has cooked for you.

249. If you must leave home unexpectedly, leave a note telling where you have gone and when you will be back.

250. Negotiate the temperature of the house to a setting all can be comfortable with.

251. Have at least one recipe you are famous for.

252. Cook chicken and turkey to an internal temperature of 170 degrees.

253. Buy organic foods when you can and always select firm, vine-ripened tomatoes.

254. Don't keep a salt shaker on the table. It will get used too often.

255. Monitor your payroll withholdings. Don't withhold more than you would owe at tax time.

256. Don't lease a car. Buy one and keep it for at least two years after you have paid for it.

257. Always pay your bills and taxes on time.

258. Keep your membership to the auto club current.

259. Don't buy more shoes than you can wear
out before they are no longer in style.

260. Don't believe everything you read
on the Internet.

261. Tip your movers well. They will be
sore long after you have gone to sleep.

262. Remember that what your child wants to hear most is "I love you."

263. Give children discipline firmly and fairly—and always with love.

264. Require your teenagers to get summer jobs. It builds character.

265. Do not shelter your children too much lest they go hog wild when they leave home.

266. Observe the maximum weight limit of ladders.

267. Learn how to administer CPR.

268. Keep a well-stocked first-aid kit on hand.

269. Learn how to handle minor injuries.

270. Pay a professional to clean your gutters.

271. Learn how to treat common childhood illnesses.

272. Do not let your insurance coverage lapse.

273. Stay calm during a crisis.

274. Love knows no schedule. Be patient. Seize it when it comes along.

275. Remain faithful to your spouse— you promised you would.

276. Leave notes of love and affection for those who will miss you when you are away.

277. Wear your heart on your sleeve. Love isn't meant to be kept secret.

278. Never let the words "I told you so" leave your mouth.

279. Don't tell those embarrassing stories if someone's feelings will be hurt.

280. Remember that sarcasm isn't funny unless it is on a stage.

281. Do not become too proud to apologize more than once now and then.

282. Know what self-righteousness sounds like and don't sound like that.

283. Offer tissue when you happen upon someone who is crying, then offer your shoulder.

284. Do not hesitate to say, "I do not understand," when you don't.

285. If you said you would, do. If you said you wouldn't, don't.

286. Try to be the first out of bed now and then to ready the day for everyone else.

287. Begin your day with a hearty, healthy breakfast.

288. Read the Sunday paper on the front porch. Wave at your neighbors as they come and go.

289. Avoid caffeine after 8 p.m.

290. Learn a few basic survival skills. You never know when you might need them.

291. If you own a gun, keep it and the ammunition in different locations.

292. Keep receipts until the warranty has expired.

293. Use a credit card when paying for repairs of any kind. It gives you leverage if things don't turn out as they should.

294. Alter your pants for your waist size today, not what you hope it will be one day.

295. Get enough sleep.

296. Always use the spell checker before you send an e-mail.

297. Play it safe most of the time but take calculated risks now and then.

298. Live by this creed: no one is beneath you.

299. Know your limits. Don't overindulge in anything.

300. Do not feed a hunger if you know you will regret it later.

301. When someone ends a talk with "Any questions?" ask one.

302. Be a reasonable skeptic, not an absolute contrarian.

303. Don't be fooled by statistics.

304. If you think you need a nap,
take one.

305. Hire a kid in the neighborhood
to do your yard work. He's probably saving
for something.

306. Keep your favorite letters and cards in
your nightstand to read when you cannot sleep.

307. Only use a walk-up ATM if it is in a
well-trafficked area and it's still daylight.

308. Never walk alone in the dark.

309. Make sure your exterior doors
are fitted with double-cylinder deadbolts.

310. Keep a fire extinguisher in your kitchen.
Replace or service it as needed.

311. Before using a drive-up ATM, make sure your doors are locked. Keep the car running.

312. Never drive through more than six inches of moving water.

313. Never let on that you are at home alone.

314. Don't ignore the warning lights in your car.

315. Learn how to check your oil and coolant levels.

316. Control your temper—on and off the road.

317. Exercise caution when driving through a parking lot.

318. Your horn is not a musical instrument. Use it only when necessary.

319. Don't wait too long to stop and ask for directions.

320. Remember that driving is not a competitive sport.

321. Practice sudden stops and recovering from running off the road. You'll be glad you did when you actually need to do it.

322. Keep your children's baby books up to date.

323. Make sure the initials of your children's names don't spell an undesirable word.

324. Don't give in just because you are tired of saying "no."

325. Don't require an apology before
forgiving someone.

326. Take care not to ask too much
from your friends.

327. Let someone know when you miss them.

328. Even if you have divided the chores, do
more than your own share.

329. If you are an expert at something,
share your knowledge with someone else.

330. Practice listening. It truly is a skill.

331. Never give your spouse or mother an appliance as a gift.

332. While you may have done most of the work, you never get anywhere all by yourself. Be sure to give thanks and credit where they are due.

333. Find an organization doing honorable work and support it with frequent donations.

334. Let your siblings know you love them. Tell them often.

335. Hold yourself to the same—or higher—standard to which you hold others.

336. Don't let a friend's last thought of you be, *I can't remember the last time we talked.*

337. Always keep the secrets others have shared with you, unless keeping that secret places them or others in harm's way.

338. Never pay cash at a going-out-of-business sale for something that must be ordered or delivered later.

339. Before buying something new, make sure you have made the best use of what you already have.

340. Buy cheap sunglasses.
It's always the expensive ones you end up losing.

341. Don't cheat on your taxes, but do everything you can to minimize your liability.

342. Use coupons whenever possible.

343. When your children want something expensive, require them to pay a portion of the cost.

344. Don't buy more house than you need, but have at least one extra bedroom for guests and grandchildren.

345. Make compound interest work for you. Start saving early. Save a lot.

346. Study days in advance of a test. You will forget too much if you wait and cram at the last minute.

347. Remember that it is better to call home and ask for a ride than it is to drive when you shouldn't.

348. Have a personal trademark. Not a weird one, but something others will remember you for.

349. Never kiss on the first date if you're not interested in a second date.

350. Hold hands in public.

351. Cuddle on a sofa with someone you love.

352. Learn how to give the perfect foot massage.

353. Date only one person at a time. It's less confusing—and cheaper.

354. Be able to throw out a good Shakespeare quote now and then.

355. Remember that although opposites attract, they seldom stay together.

356. Walk away from a fight, even one you could win.

357. Try to learn something from what others attempt to teach you. Then teach others what you have learned.

358. Be understanding of your parents' fears as they grapple with letting go of you. It is just another sign of how much they love you.

359. When in doubt, call your parents for advice.

360. Believe it—they are called "bad boys" for a reason.

361. Don't strive too hard to be unique. Others find comfort in convention. But it's okay to be a *little* wacky.

362. First dates are an audition. Always give your best, but genuine, performance if you want the part.

363. Put the windows down and enjoy the wind in your hair.

364. Laugh often, laugh with gusto.

365. Always sing along to your favorite songs. Sing loud.

366. If you live in an upstairs apartment, walk softly between 9 p.m. and 6 a.m.

367. Be on time. There is no such thing as "fashionably late."

368. If you must talk on the cell phone, go outside. No one wants to know your business.

369. Learn how to set a table and which utensil to use when.

370. Never start your mower before 9 a.m.

371. Always practice good table manners,
even if at a picnic.

372. When visiting others,
don't bring your pets along unless
they were invited, too.

373. Let *please* be one of your
most-often-used words.

374. Wear a pedometer and walk 10,000 steps a day. You will live longer.

375. Don't ignore an ingrown toenail; it won't correct itself.

376. Protect your eyes and ears. You cannot replace them.

377. Watch the local news in the morning and the national news in the evening.

378. Listen to every presidential address; read every gubernatorial statement. You should know what is going on in your government.

379. Turn off the TV at least one hour a day. Use that time for conversation or reading.

380. Know which radio station gives frequent traffic and weather reports.

381. Don't try too hard to get noticed.

382. Accept the criticism of others. You will never be perfect, your efforts never flawless.

383. Let sleeping dogs lie.

384. You cannot make someone love you, but you can make yourself someone another could love.

385. Always share the spotlight.

386. Know what brings out the worst in you and avoid it.

387. Yes, you are an individual. But don't rub it in the face of everyone you pass.

388. Monitor your children closely, but give them room to grow.

389. Make your children eat what is good for them.

390. Experience behind the wheel saves lives. Begin teaching your child how to drive as soon as you can get away with it.

391. Put things back where you found them, especially those that came from the refrigerator.

392. When estimating your time of arrival, allow some time for the unexpected.

393. Check your voicemail regularly and return all calls on a timely basis.

394. Keep an extra pen in your briefcase or purse.

395. Synchronize all the watches and clocks in your house.

396. Always save some time and energy for yourself.

397. Remember to be playful and silly once in a while, especially with children.

398. Change your routine occasionally. In doing so you will discover some new pleasures now and then.

399. When your life isn't going according to plan, ask yourself if you have the right plan.

400. When you are lost, stop; don't just keep going. Staying in one place makes it easier for others to find you.

401. Always carry a little emergency cash—but not too much.

402. When proceeding into an unfamiliar place, watch for landmarks so you can find your way back.

403. Never get into the car of a stranger or let one into yours.

404. Keep your cell phone fully charged.

405. Make sure your windows and doors are shut and locked before going to bed.

406. Spend the extra money and get high-speed Internet service. It's worth it.

407. Don't invest in a TV what you should be saving for braces.

408. Give your children an allowance and use it to teach them about budgeting.

409. Put yourself on an allowance, too.

410. When on a team, don't fall back and hide among the others. Work harder to get noticed.

411. Never stop at "good enough." Continue until you get to "as good as possible."

412. Don't sweat the small stuff. There will be plenty of big stuff to sweat over.

413. If you broke or lost something you borrowed, replace it with something better.

414. Be intolerant of intolerance.

415. Don't try to cure an alcoholic or drug addict. They must do it for themselves.

416. Maintain eye contact when in serious conversations.

417. Don't blame others for something that is your own fault.

418. Base your exercise program on the FIT Principle—as Frequent as possible, as Intense as possible, and for as much Time as possible.

419. Wear flip-flops when using a public shower.

420. Don't ignore your body. If something doesn't seem right, go see a doctor.

421. Try alternative medicine for your aches and pains. It works.

422. Get a second opinion before agreeing to have surgery.

423. Use surge protectors on your expensive electronic equipment.

424. Make sure there is a Bible, a dictionary, a thesaurus, a clock, and a jar for loose change in your house.

425. Blow out burning candles before leaving a room.

426. Maintain your computer's health.
Use virus protection software and defrag
the hard drive often.

427. Never give personal identification data to
anyone you don't know.

428. Write down on the chart of the fuse box
door what each fuse controls.

429. Buy the safest car you can afford,
not the most stylish one.

430. Go back home and visit once in a while. Your loved ones miss you when you are away.

431. Let your parents indulge their grandchildren.

432. Always treat your in-laws with warm respect.

433. Let your faith guide your most difficult decisions.

434. Use scripture to manage yourself, not others.

435. Keep an umbrella in your car.

436. Travel with breath mints. You never know when you may need one.

437. Make sure you keep a cell phone charger in your glove box.

438. Buy the best tires you can afford.

439. Replace your windshield wipers when needed. It is important to be able to see clearly.

440. Learn and obey all traffic laws.

441. Always park in a well-lit, conspicuous place.

442. Always travel with your car doors locked.

443. When you hear unusual noises, investigate them sooner rather than later.

444. Slow down when approaching a school zone.

445. Routinely check to make sure all the lights of your car are working.

446. Don't park so close to another car that you can't get in and out easily. Everyone needs a little space.

447. Memorize your car's tag number.

448. Pour your coffee into a carafe to keep it warm instead of letting it sit on the burner. It will taste better longer.

449. Eat where the locals, not the tourists, eat.

450. Experiment with eating ethnic foods.

451. Always add a few bay leaves to the pot when cooking beans.

452. Check the expiration date on everything in your kitchen before eating it.

453. Keep a box of cookie or cake mix in the pantry.

454. Meet your neighbors and say hello to them every time you see them.

455. Keep a welcome mat at your front door.

456. Strike up a conversation with the cab driver.

457. Become friendly with those who work at places you frequent.

458. Always be polite to your dry cleaner and barber.

459. Never turn down an offer to dance or the chance to ask someone to dance.

460. Attend all your high school reunions.

461. Save mementos from special occasions.

462. Make a party out of decorating the Christmas tree.

463. Watch *It's a Wonderful Life* every Christmas.

464. Be willing to change your plans when something more important comes along.

465. If something is important to you, be persistent in pursuing it. The next try may be the one that works.

466. Think twice before becoming a public figure. You may lose your privacy.

467. Recognize when someone cannot deviate from company policy to satisfy you. Don't berate them but do take your complaint to a higher authority.

468. Stand up for your consumer rights. Don't allow yourself to be taken advantage of but at the same time be reasonable.

469. Always give two weeks' notice when leaving a job and give your best effort during those two weeks.

470. If you don't respect your boss, quit your job—but not before you have a new one.

471. Choose a prominent wall in your home and cover it with pictures of your family.

472. Buy moderately priced wines to get the best value for your dollar.

473. Learn how to eat with chopsticks.

474. Restaurant portions are often huge. Eat only half and take the rest home for lunch tomorrow.

475. Don't spend your money on seldom-used kitchen gadgets but do splurge on good pots and pans.

476. Know how to select a fresh fish at the market.

477. Never let a waiter intimidate you.

478. Always review your check before paying for the meal.

479. Balance your checkbook each month
to the penny.

480. Don't put more on a credit card than you
can pay for in ninety days.

481. Never cosign a loan with anyone other
than your spouse and children.

482. Never lend more money than you would
be willing to give as a gift in the first place.

483. Resist the temptation to increase your standard of living with every pay raise.

484. Keep a little room in the budget for the unexpected.

485. Change your PIN and passwords often. Share them with no one but your spouse.

486. Although there is an exception to every rule, it should seldom apply to you.

487. Control yourself, not others.

488. Play fair, but use the rules to your advantage.

489. Recognize that it isn't possible to be right all the time.

490. Be a humble winner and a gracious loser.

491. Think before you speak. Words cannot be taken back.

492. A gentle touch makes a powerful statement. Touch often.

493. Never fail to say, "I love you, too."

494. Let compassion be something you are known for.

495. Be supportive of your spouse through all of his or her endeavors.

496. Take a drive through the countryside and appreciate what God has made.

497. Believe in miracles. They really do occur.

498. Leave a legacy that inspires.

499. Life is much like a road trip. Plan ahead and be safe. Enjoy the journey.

500. Always remember your way home.

Acknowledgments

In this book about finding your way in life, I wish to say thanks to some of those who have given me love, support, direction, and encouragement along my journey—Gene and Dianne Lang, Stanley Brown, Eddie Brown, Mary Jean Register, Elaine Brown, Jimmy and Sandra Kennedy, O. L. Brown, John Buhman, Dan Donovan, Al Kramer, Lisa McGillem, Nancy Mudd, Missy Crawford, Alistair Deakin, Dave and Joan Kersys, Rick Simon, Pat Bickley, Ron Pitkin, Lisa Taylor, Janet Moran, Greg Crawford, Ann Beard, Luanna Hinson, Richard Endsley, Karen Wampler, Jim and Linda Walters, Trisha Ruppersberg, Harold Lee, Evie Crumbliss, Lee Perdue, Vicki Kowlowitz, Barbara Sheppard, Sam Hutto, Peter Brown, Joanna Watson, Ruth Slentz, T. P. Haines, Cindy Zeagler-Stevens, Patricia DeBary, Elaine Benefield, John O'Kelley, Melissa Cianciotti, Ruthie Blue Sky, Patricia Leaptrot, Johnny and Joann Parris, and my incredible-beyond-my-wildest-dreams wife, Jill Lang.

TO CONTACT THE AUTHOR

write in care of the publisher:
Cumberland House Publishing
431 Harding Industrial Drive
Nashville, TN 37211

or e-mail:
greg.lang@mindspring.com